Acknowledgements

Thanks are due to Janet Ford, Sarah Nettleton and Christine Oldman for useful comments on earlier drafts of this report. Thanks are also due to Jane Allen and Sue Anscombe for preparing the final version.

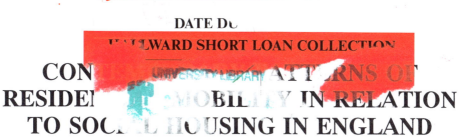

CONTEMPORARY PATTERNS OF RESIDENTIAL MOBILITY IN RELATION TO SOCIAL HOUSING IN ENGLAND

Roger Burrows

RESEARCH REPORT

CENTRE FOR HOUSING POLICY
University of York

Published by:
Centre for Housing Policy
University of York
York YO1 5DD
Telephone 01904 433691
Fax 01904 432318

ISBN 1 874797 77 3

Typeset by Sue Anscombe in the Centre for Housing Policy
Printed by York Publishing Services Ltd

The **Joseph Rowntree Foundation** has supported this project as part of its programme of research and innovative development projects, which it hopes will be of value to policy makers and practitioners. The facts presented and views expressed in this report however, are those of the authors and not necessarily those of the Foundation.

Contents

List of tables and figures

Appendix:

Introduction

This short report summarises some of the key findings from an investigation into patterns of residential mobility in relation to social housing in England derived from a secondary analysis of the *1993/4 Survey of English Housing (SEH)*. Chapter 1 sets the context for the research and also briefly describes how some of the central variables have been measured. It also provides a 'conceptual map' of the patterns of residential mobility which are explored in the subsequent Chapters. Chapter 2 examines patterns of residential mobility within the social rented sector by households with continuing heads of household (as defined in Chapter 1). Chapter 3 examines movements between the owner occupied sector and social housing by households with continuing heads of household. Chapter 4 examines movements between the private rented sector and social housing by households with continuing heads of household. Chapter 5 considers some of the characteristics of new households (as defined in Chapter 1) entering the social rented sector. Finally, Chapter 6 offers some brief concluding remarks on the analysis.

Chapter One
Residential mobility in relation to social housing in England: setting the context

Introduction

There has been a longstanding interest in patterns of residential mobility in the British social sciences.[1] The reasons for this interest are not difficult to fathom. First, residential mobility is concerned with the relationship between structure and agency, the core topic of much contemporary *social theory*. As Buck (1996: 1) views it, residential mobility raises questions of:

> how structural factors influence individual behaviour...the influence of past events in the individual's life course on current behaviour and...how structures are modified by the accumulation of individual behaviours.

Second, residential mobility raises a whole set of technical research issues so beloved by social statisticians and others with a fetish for *methodology*. Third, and most importantly, an understanding of patterns of residential mobility is central to a whole gamut of *social and public policy issues*.

Hitherto, however, much of the policy literature on residential mobility has been dominated by concerns with the relationship between housing provision and the mobility of labour.[2] Although this is obviously an important topic, such a concentration on this theme has led to some other issues receiving less attention than they might deserve. Annual rates of household residential mobility in England have varied between 9 and 11 per cent of the total number of households in England since 1981 (Green *et al.*, 1996: 230) - a proportion which represented some 2.1 million separate household moves in 1993/4 - and although a proportion of these moves will be due to labour market factors,

---

[1]   For an excellent review of this voluminous literature see Champion and Fielding (1992) and Forrest *et al.* (1991).

[2]   For an overview of this literature see Forrest *et al.* (1991) and Forrest and Murie (1992). An example of recent work in this area is Boyle (1995).

a large proportion will be a function of a range of other socio-economic, cultural and demographic variables.

The focus of the study reported here is on contemporary patterns of residential mobility in relation to social housing in England. Although the influence of the labour market on patterns of mobility will be considered, it does not form the primary emphasis of the work. Rather, the research attempts to map out the overall *pattern* and, where possible, the *causes* of residential mobility amongst a population increasingly *excluded* from the formal labour market.[3] There are at least two reasons why this is an important undertaking.

First, there is an oft-cited view that tenant mobility has declined in England in the 1990s as the local authority stock has reduced and letting pressures have increased. However, recent research by Maclennan and Kay (1994) has concluded that this might not be the case. Indeed, there is good evidence to suggest that as it has become smaller the rate of residential mobility within the social rented sector has increased. As we shall see, in 1984 the total number of moves within the sector represented about 4.2 per cent of the total number of local authority and housing association dwellings, whilst in 1993/4 they represented 6.9 per cent. This increased rate of mobility is due to a number of factors, but is primarily a result of the demographic profile of tenants in the social rented sector. The age distribution of heads of household in the social rented sector in 1993/94 is shown in Figure 1.1. Almost 38 per cent of all existing heads of household in the social rented sector are aged 65 or over and 19 per cent are aged 75 or over. The increasing number of deaths due to the ageing of this population has made mobility within the sector possible despite its overall decrease in size. As the rate of mobility within the social rented sector increases, the stability in tenant populations necessary for sustainable community development is potentially undermined (Page, 1993; Power, 1994; Power and Tunstall, 1995). As well as raising issues concerned with the building and maintaining of communities, such an increase in the rate of residential mobility also has major implications for the management of social housing (Maclennan and Kay, 1994; Bines *et al.*, 1993), not least increased costs.[4]

---

[3]   Overviews of the literature on social housing and social exclusion in Britain are provided in Lee *et al.* (1995).

[4]   This observed increase in the rate of 'churning' within the social rented sector also touches upon issues raised by recent research which has begun to indicate the increasing importance of local mobility amongst younger (usually male) members of disadvantaged communities. This new *nomadism* is as yet little understood but has been hinted at within a number of recent small scale studies (Campbell, 1993: 166-187; Carlen, 1996; Speak *et al.*, 1995; Vincent *et al.*, 1993) and in contemporary social and cultural theory (Featherstone, 1995; Lash and Urry, 1994).

Figure 1.1
The Age Distribution of Heads of Household in the Social Rented Sector 1993/4 ('000s)

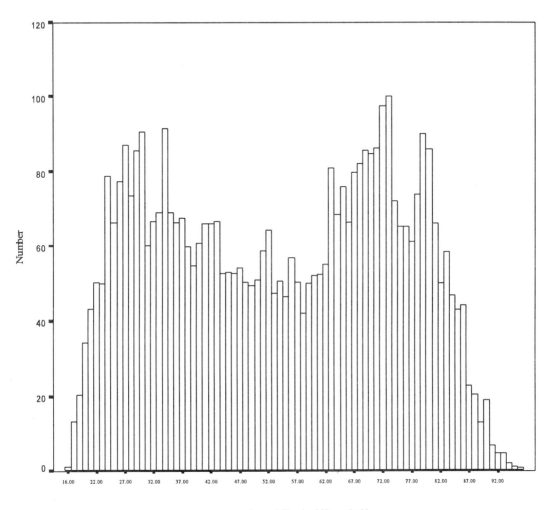

Age of Head of Household

Second, flows of individuals, families and households between and within the different tenures contribute to the widely documented and continuing process of *residualisation* within social housing. The evidence is that differences in the socio-economic characteristics of those entering (Prescott-Clarke *et al.*, 1994) compared to those leaving the social rented sector are resulting in social housing becoming more narrowly based socially and economically (Forrest and Murie, 1990b; Power, 1994; Power and Tunstall, 1995). An analysis of residential mobility in relation to social housing thus provides an insight into the *dynamics* of residualisation. Hitherto, much of the analysis of residualisation has, quite properly, concentrated on the operation of the *Right to Buy* (RTB) legislation (Forrest and Murie, 1983; 1990a; 1990b; 1994a) in the process of social exclusion. Between 1980 and 1994 a total of some 1,246,830 dwellings in England were transferred from the social rented sector to owner occupation (Wilcox, 1995: 103). The characteristics of the bulk of exiting purchasers resulted in a markedly changed socio-economic profile in the remaining social housing population (Forrest and Murie, 1990a; Wilcox, 1995: 113-121). However, the process of residualisation has not just been due to changes in the tenure of *dwellings*, it has also been due to the intensification of processes of residential movement by *people* which can be traced back to at least the mid-1970s as those able to do so have left the sector and entered owner occupation (Lee *et al.*, 1995: 27). The research reported here might thus be viewed as a useful supplement to recent work carried out by the Institute of Fiscal Studies (1996). This work has concluded that it:

> is not, by and large, the case that a group of people - those in the social sector - remained in the same sector and became poorer over time...Rather what has happened is that the composition of the sector has changed. Those who could afford to have moved out, those who couldn't have stayed behind. And those newly entering the sector have been especially poor... (IFS, 1996: 1).

An analysis of residential mobility thus provides us with an insight into changes at the 'margin' of each tenure which in turn gives us an indication of the 'tendency' or 'direction' of social change within each tenure (Burrows, 1997b; Watt, 1996). As such the analysis informs contemporary debates concerning housing and social exclusion.

Residential mobility and social exclusion

The analysis presented here is written at a different level of abstraction to other recent studies of mobility such as those carried out by Durrant and Taper (1995), Maclennan and Kay (1994) and Prescott-Clarke *et al.* (1994). These studies have been primarily concerned with the institutional and organisational arrangements through which residential movement into and within social housing occurs, whereas this report is primarily concerned to describe the complex patterns of movement which these arrangements underpin. The analysis which follows shows that there

> continues to be a very clear funnelling of those affected by unemployment, labour market change, low incomes, relationship breakdown, family disputes, homelessness and unsatisfactory and insecure housing towards the social rented sector.
>
> (Lee *et al.*, 1995: 45)

As tenancies become available in the social rented sector the population superseding older more established tenants are, on average, significantly younger. Not only this but (not surprisingly) they are far more likely to have children and far more likely to be headed by someone who is unemployed or unable to work (although, because of their age profile, far less likely to be retired). Households headed by someone who is economically active are significantly more likely to 'exit' social housing for owner occupation or to move within the social rented sector to accommodation they intend to purchase through the RTB.

Overwhelmingly then, the social housing which remains post-RTB is being populated by individuals and households who are increasingly socially excluded (Room, 1995). The various theoretical debates which surround the concept of social exclusion need not detain us here. All we need note is that as a concept what differentiates it from more 'traditional' concepts such as 'poverty' or 'deprivation' is that it gives an emphasis to the understanding of the socio-economic *dynamics* of the *processes* by which different groups of people are more or less dis/advantaged. Thus, any framework informed by the idea of social exclusion in relation to housing automatically focuses upon the mechanisms and processes which (over both time and space) sift and sort people into more or less favourable housing situations. Although these mechanisms and processes are many and varied, in the last instance it is the *physical mobility* of individuals and households which comes to define an area and the community which occupies it. Thus any description of patterns of residential mobility is also, at one and the same time, a description of the social restructuring of places.

If the characteristics of households entering an area mirror the characteristics of those leaving it, existing patterns of cultural and socio-economic relations will tend to be reproduced. If, however, the characteristics of those entering an area significantly differ from the characteristics of those households leaving it, then cultural and socio-economic relations will tend to change.

Two different examples illustrate this point well. First, in relation to owner occupation, the temporal and spatial process of what came to be known as 'gentrification' represents the middle class colonization of areas and the consequent exclusion of non-middle class residents (Butler, 1995). Second, in relation to social housing, Power (1994: 11) has identified a clear process by which a 'lettings spiral' leads some council estates to have a much higher concentration of social problems than other areas. These different and shifting patterns of the social composition of areas are of course related, in that exclusion from one zone means displacement into another. In the final analysis it is largely through long term aggregate patterns of residential mobility that the social structures of our villages, towns and cities come about.

If one approaches the analysis contained within this report using this sort of framework, then, as already stated, it becomes possible to think about patterns of household movement as indicators of the 'direction' or 'tendency' of social change within social housing in England. Although the data we have relied on here is not detailed enough to examine how these processes manifest themselves within any particular locality[5], it does allow us to form a view about processes of change at a national level.

Data Source

The research reported here is based upon an extensive secondary analysis of the *Survey of English Housing* (SEH) for 1993/4[6] (Green and Hansbro, 1995; Green *et al.*, 1996). The SEH is a continuous government survey which began in April 1993. It is based upon interviews with about 20,000 households in England each year. It has two distinct aims. First, to provide data on tenure, owner occupation and the social rented sector, where regular monitoring is needed. The main source of data in the past was a supplementary questionnaire ('housing trailer') attached to the Labour Force Survey (LFS) (DoE, 1993). Second, to provide regular data about the private rented sector. In the past, private renters have had to be examined by means of *ad hoc* surveys based on samples identified from the LFS. Details of the sample design, data collection, response rates and so on are detailed in annual reports (Green and Hansbro, 1995; Green *et al.*, 1996). The SEH provides an annual nationally representative sample of a good size and covers a wide range of topics relating to housing circumstances, household structure and a host of socio-economic variables.

Conceptualising residential mobility in relation to social housing

One of the great advantages of research designs based upon the secondary analysis of large and complex data sets is that an enormous amount of useful and interesting data can be generated. However, this can also be a disadvantage in that the amount of information

---

[5]   But see Power and Tunstall (1995) for excellent locality based data.

[6]   Material from the SEH was made available through the Office of National Statistics and the ESRC Data Archive with the permission of the Controller of H.M. Stationary Office. The microdata for the 1994/5 SEH only became available through the Data Archive in September 1996 not allowing time for any full secondary analysis. However, at certain points in this report the 1994/5 data is referred to when results from the published report (Green *et al.*, 1996) and initial work on the data files by the author contradict and/or supplement the data from 1993/4.

it is possible to produce can become so great that analytic clarity can easily be lost under the weight of empirical material. It is therefore especially important that both the analysis and presentation of such data is organised in terms of a clear conceptual framework.

The focus of this report is on the characteristics of the flows of households and individuals *within* and *between* social housing and the other main tenures - owner occupation and the private rented sector (PRS).

By the notion of *residential mobility* is meant:

▸ any move in place of usual residence, regardless of distance, that has occurred in the 12 months prior to interview.

Moves may be made by *households* of two different types:

▸ by *wholly moving households* or *continuing households* where the household structure and, consequently, the head of household does not change.

▸ by *new households* formed by individuals who were previously 'nested' within (one or more) other households, such as adult children leaving the parental home or couples separating and living as single persons or forming new partnerships.

This means that there are, logically, eight mutually exclusive sets of household flows within and between the three main tenures[7]. These different sets of flows are used as a basis for describing patterns of mobility throughout the rest of the report. A brief summary of some of the main characteristics of these flows are given below. They are shown diagrammatically in Figure 1.2.

---

[7] In most cases data on previous tenure is reliably collected in the SEH. However for married or cohabiting couples this information was collected from the household head if he moved in first or both partners had moved in together. In a small number of cases the partner moved in first, and previous tenure was not asked of her. In order to maintain comparability with data from previous surveys, tenure information for the head of household was imputed for these cases (Green and Hansbro, 1995).

Figure 1.2
Conceptualising Patterns of Residential Mobility in Relation to Social Housing

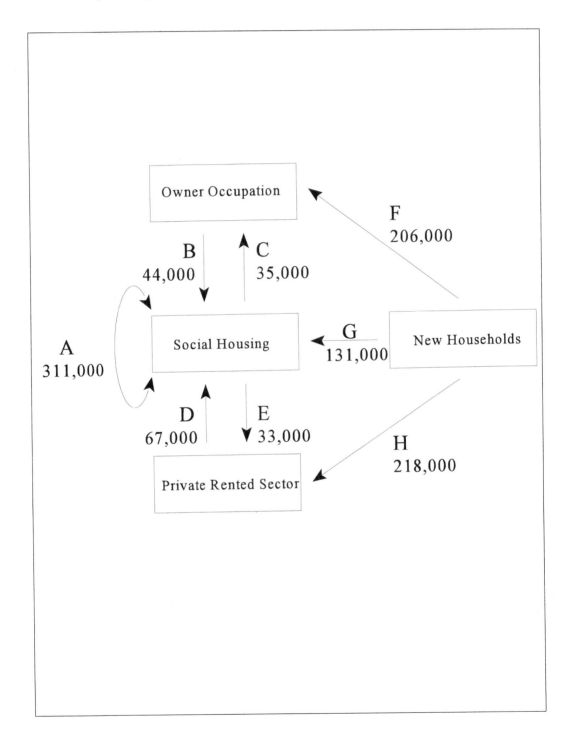

Residential mobility within the social rented sector

The recursive flow of households marked 'A' represents movements *within* the social rented sector by continuing wholly moving households. These may be moves within or between local authority housing and/or housing association accommodation.[8] In 1984, 1988 and 1991 (the years for which data is available) such household moves represented about 12 per cent of all household moves in England in each year (Green and Hansbro, 1995: 181-182). However, in 1993/4 such moves represented 14.6 per cent of all household moves, a total of some 311 thousand moves in the year.[9]

In addition, as the size of the social rented stock has been decreasing during this period, from 5,134 thousand dwellings in 1984 to 4,495 thousand dwellings in 1994 (Wilcox, 1995: 92), the rate of residential mobility within the social rented sector has been increasing relatively as well as absolutely. In 1984 moves within the social rented sector represented 4.2 per cent of the total number of local authority and housing association dwellings, whilst in 1993/4 they represented some 6.9 per cent.[10]

Residential mobility between owner occupation and the social rented sector

The flows of households marked 'B' and 'C' represent movements between the social rented sector and owner occupation by continuing wholly moving households. Moves between these two types of tenure by continuing households generally constitute between 3 and 4 per cent of all household moves within any one year. In both 1984 and 1988 the balance of these flows represented a net outflow into owner occupation from the social rented sector. However, following the housing recession of the late 1980s and 1990s (Forrest and Murie, 1994b; Ford, 1997) the balance of movement altered. In 1991 the balance represented a net inflow of some 19 thousand households into social housing from owner occupation (Green and Hansbro, 1995: 181-182). The SEH data for 1993/4 suggests

---

[8]   In order to maintain clarity within Figure 1.2 these two types of social renting are collapsed into one category - social housing. In Chapter 2 the pattern of mobility within and between local authority and housing association accommodation is briefly discussed but the small number of cases preclude any systematic investigation of variations between the two.

[9]   Since the sample is roughly based upon one in one thousand households each household in the sample can be multiplied by one thousand to give an estimate of the number of households in England.

[10]   However, the figures from the 1994/5 SEH suggest a decrease in the number of such household moves from 311 thousand to 271 thousand, representing some 12.8 per cent of all household moves and just over 6 per cent of the total number of local authority and housing association dwellings.

a continuation of this movement with some 44 thousand households entering social housing from owner occupation and some 35 thousand households leaving the social rented sector and entering owner occupation (a net inflow of some 9 thousand households) (Green and Hansbro, 1995: 181).[11]

Residential mobility between the private rented sector and the social rented sector

The flows of households marked 'D' and 'E' represent movements between the social rented sector and the private rented sector by continuing wholly moving households. Moves between these two types of tenure by continuing households constitute between 4 and 5 per cent of all household moves within any one year. In every year for which there is data there has been a net inflow from the private rented sector to the social rented sector. The size of the balance fluctuates across time and no clear trends are decipherable. In 1993/4 some 33 thousand continuing households left the social rented sector and entered the private rented sector, whilst some 67 thousand continuing households left the private rented sector and entered the social rented sector - a net inflow of some 29 thousand continuing households.

The residential mobility of new households

The flows of households marked 'F', 'G' and 'H' represent the residential movements of new households. Of the 2.1 million household moves in 1993/4 about 26 per cent (0.6 million) were made by new households. The number of new households formed in any one year fluctuates year on year but there are some indications of a secular decline in the number of new households being formed between 1988 and 1994. In 1988 some 637 thousand new households were formed in England but by 1993/4 the number had fallen to 555 thousand, 131 thousand of whom entered social housing. One explanation for this decrease may be that younger people are continuing to live with parents rather than moving into a home of their own (Holmans, 1996). Another explanation is the fall in the number of young adults. In 1988 there were 3.8 million 20 to 24 year olds, but in 1993 just 3.5 million (Green and Hansbro, 1995: 85).

These new households were previously 'nested' within other households. Although the SEH data provides details of the current characteristics of new households, it does not

---

[11]   However, the SEH data for 1994/5 suggests a possible reversal of this trend with just 27 thousand households entering social housing from owner occupation whilst 38 thousand households left the social rented sector to enter owner occupation (a net outflow of some 11 thousand households) (Green *et al.*, 1996: 231).

contain very much information about how they were constituted or where they came from. However, it is possible to get some estimates of this from the British Household Panel Survey (BHPS). Published data from the first two waves of the BHPS suggested that 40.4 per cent of new households were formed by 'children' leaving the parental home, 17.2 per cent were created by separating couples and 42.4 per cent were new households formed by new configurations of individuals headed by someone who had not previously been a head of household (mostly from within the private rented sector).[12]

Obviously these new households do not appear out of a tenurial ether. They were all previously 'nested' within other households located within one or other type of tenure. The BHPS data suggests that of all new households formed, some 15 per cent were, prior to moving, living in other households located in the social rented sector. Of these new households from the social rented sector almost 29 per cent moved into owner occupation, 50 per cent remained in social housing and just over 21 per cent moved into the private rented sector. The BHPS data suggest that these figures represent just over 7 per cent of all new households entering owner occupation, almost 52 per cent of all new households entering the social rented sector and just over 6 per cent of all new households entering the private rented sector. These movements explain the necessity for three household flows in the diagram in order to represent the full pattern of residential mobility flows of new households in relation to social housing. However, in this report we only examine flow 'G' which represents new households moving into social housing

Summary

This Chapter has outlined some reasons why an analysis of contemporary patterns of residential mobility in relation to social housing is important. It has also described the data source, the 1993/4 *Survey of English Housing*, upon which the rest of the report is based. It has formally defined residential mobility as any move in place of usual residence, regardless of distance, that has occurred in the 12 months prior to interview and has drawn a conceptual distinction between moves by *continuing* wholly moving households and *new* households. It has defined the scope of the study in terms of a set of eight household flows within and between the social rented sector and the other main tenures and has provided a brief statistical sketch of each set of movements using data from the SEH and the BHPS. The task of the following Chapters is to examine the nature of each of these sets of movements in more detail.

---

[12]   These figures from the BHPS and the ones which follow in this section have been calculated from the data provided in Table 6.3 of Buck (1994: 138).

Chapter Two
Patterns of residential mobility amongst continuing households within the social rented sector

Introduction

This Chapter describes the pattern of residential mobility amongst continuing households within the social rented sector - that is, movements within both local authority and housing association stock. Data from the SEH 1993/4 suggests that some 311 thousand such moves took place in the year. Table 2.1 shows how these moves were distributed within and between the two sectors.

Table 2.1
Movements within the social rented sector within and between local authority and housing association stock by continuing households

	Previous tenure local authority	Previous tenure housing association	N
Current tenure local authority	222,000	10,000	232,000
Current tenure housing association	29,000	50,000	79,000
N	251,000	60,000	311,000

The majority of moves, some 222 thousand (71.4 per cent), were movements within the local authority stock. Some 50 thousand moves (16.1 per cent) were movements within the housing association sector. Some 29 thousand moves (9.3 per cent) were movements out of local authority housing into housing association accommodation and just 10 thousand (3.2 per cent) were moves in the opposite direction.

It would be interesting to examine if the household characteristics and the reasons and motivations for mobility differed between these four different types of move within the social rented sector. However, the small number of cases in the SEH preclude any meaningful analysis.[13] Instead in this Chapter we shall examine two aspects of mobility within the sector as a whole. First, we shall investigate if there are any identifiable characteristics which differentiate moving continuing households from all other (non moving) households in the social rented sector as a whole. Second, we shall describe the characteristics and the motivations of moving households.

Do continuing household movers within the social rented sector differ from the rest of the social rented tenant population?

In order to answer this question satisfactorily we need to utilise multivariate statistics. Unfortunately all too often the use of such analytic tools in the social and policy sciences obscure more than they reveal. This is a great pity because it is often the case that multivariate analysis is the most appropriate framework within which to understand complex social processes. Such is the case here. As we draw upon the same multivariate method to examine patterns of residential mobility at a number of points in the analysis which follows it is worth outlining the approach taken in some detail. This is provided in an Appendix to the report and draws upon the data on mobility within social housing discussed here. It is strongly suggested that readers unfamiliar with logistic regression techniques read the Appendix.

Following the procedures outlined in the Appendix a wide range of demographic and socio-economic variables, which on *a priori* grounds were suspected to be associated with residential mobility, were examined. Of all of those examined a total of six different variables were found to demonstrate some form of bivariate association with the odds of being mobile: current employment status of the head of household; type of household structure; the social class of the head of household; the age of the head of household; the ethnicity of the head of household; and region. A categorical version of the age variable was found to fit more satisfactorily than a continuous version and through processes of trial and error variables were collapsed in theoretically coherent ways when it made sense to do so. In addition to the influence of individual variables a range of 'interaction' effects were also tested for. An assessment was made of the combination of these variables which 'best fitted' the data using standard methods of model selection. Of the six variables

---

[13]   It is possible to do some limited analysis by combining SEH data for two years but this still only generates a small number of cases for moves between local authority and housing association dwellings.

which demonstrated some form of bivariate association only four were required in the 'best fitting' model. When other factors were controlled for, the influence of the ethnicity and social class background of the head of household was no longer significant. The final 'best fitting' model is shown in Table 2.2.

What does this model mean? It suggests that there are some distinct socio-demographic factors which predispose some households within the social rented sector to be residentially mobile within the social rented sector. The model contains four variables - two of which operate on their own and two of which only 'act' in 'interaction' with each other.

Table 2.2
'Best fitting' logistic regression model of the odds of
continuing households being mobile within the social rented sector

Variable	'Best fitting'
Base odds	0.17
Age of head of household	
16-29	1.00
30-44	0.42***
45-54	0.35***
55-64	0.31***
65-74	0.19***
75+	0.17***
Region	
North	1.10
Yorks & Humber	0.70
East Midlands	1.46
East Anglia	1.45
Greater London	0.88
Rest of South East	0.76
South West	1.78**
West Midlands	0.91
North West	1.04
Current employment status of the HoH* type of household structure (Interaction)	
Not	1.00
Eco Inactive x couples with dependent children	1.80**
Eco Inactive x lone parents with dependent children	1.74**

** sig. at p<0.01) *** sig. at p<0.001
R_L^2 = 8.1% Model Chi-Square = 148.9, sig at p<0.001 for the 'best fitting' model.

First, the model suggests that, after controlling for the effects of region, current employment status and household structure, the odds of moving decrease with age. Second, the model suggests that, after controlling for age, current employment status and household structure, the only region in England where the odds of mobility are significantly increased is in the South West. The variable for region is treated in a slightly different manner to the other variables in the model. The contrasts between the categories are calculated in relation to the overall effect of region on the odds of mobility and not in relation to some arbitrary reference category. Essentially this means that the effect of each region is being contrasted with the mean effect of all regions. This means that we can identify any regions within which mobility is significantly more or less likely compared to England as a whole. Finally, the model suggests that there is a significant 'interaction' effect between the employment status of the head of household and household structure. After controlling for age and region amongst those who are economically inactive the odds of moving are significantly increased in households with dependent children.

The model can be interpreted as follows. The figure for the 'base odds' is the estimate of the odds of moving for a household with the combined characteristics of the 'reference' categories of each variable (the top category within each variable with an odds estimate set at 1.00 for all variables except region where the comparison is with England as a whole rather than any particular regional category). In this case this refers to households without dependent children with an economically inactive head of household who is aged between 16 and 29 located anywhere in England. Each odds estimate refers to how changing the characteristics of the household increases or decreases the chances of the household moving. So for instance if the household were in the South West the model estimates that the odds of moving would be significantly increased by a factor of 1.78 (i.e. 0.17 x 1.78 = 0.30). If the head of household were aged between 30 and 44 the odds of moving would be decreased by a factor of 0.42. If the head of household were an economically inactive lone parent the odds would increase by a factor of 1.74. The model suggest then that the household type most likely to move within the social rented sector is one with an economically inactive lone parent as head of household aged between 16 and 29 living in the South West of England.

The characteristics of continuing households who have moved within the social rented sector and their reasons for moving

Logistic regression analysis allows us to model the odds of different types of household being mobile but it does not tell us very much about the absolute number of households of different types moving. It is therefore important to describe the characteristics of the households who have actually moved and also to understand some of their motivations for moving. Although the odds of older households moving are less than for younger households, the fact that 51.4 per cent of heads of household in the social rented sector are aged 55 years or over means that in absolute terms a large number of older households actually move.

Data on the continuing households mobile within the social rented sector are shown in Table 2.3 (overleaf). The Table classifies the households into eight different types on the basis of the current economic activity of the head of household and the structure of the household: single person households; other households without dependent children; couples with dependent children; and lone parents with dependent children. Although dividing up the moving households in this way leads to some small cell counts, it does allow some clear differences between the households to be examined.

The Table is complex because it summarises much information. Each cell shows the number of households with the particular combination of characteristics and also what this number represents proportionately in terms of all households. Each cell also contains data on: the mean age of the head of household; the two main reasons given for moving by households of the type represented by the cell, ranked in order; the proportion of such households who say that they intend to try and purchase the property into which they have recently moved; the three most common 'routes' into the new tenancy ranked in order; and the median distance the move into the new accommodation represented.

Table 2.3 shows that single person households are the most common type of household amongst movers. They represent over 30 per cent of all continuing households moving within the social rented sector. The great majority (over 82 per cent) of moving single person households are economically inactive and old (with a mean age of over 55 years - the oldest mean age of all the household types). Of the minority who are economically active (21.3 per cent) the main motivations for moving were to live in a 'better area' (32 per cent) followed by divorce or separation (17 per cent). Whilst amongst the older economically inactive movers the main motivations were 'family reasons' followed by a desire for more suitable accommodation.[14]

---

[14]   The label 'larger/better house' used in the SEH is not very helpful as it conflates issues of the size of accommodation with an evaluation of its quality. It is clear from the pattern of responses that it is probably best to interpret the meaning of this response as 'more appropriate accommodation'. This is the term which is therefore used in the text when referring to this response.

Table 2.3
The characteristics of continuing households moving within the social rented sector

	Head of household is economically active		Head of household is economically inactive		Totals
Single people	17		77		94
Row %	17.9%		82.1%		100.0%
Column %	21.3%		33.5%		30.1%
Mean age of HoH	36.6		55.2		
Main reasons for move	1 better area	32%	1 family reasons	25%	
	2 divorce/separation	17%	2 larger/better house	16%	
% Intending to buy	23%		4%		
How started renting?	1 waiting/transfer list	64%	1 waiting/transfer list	60%	
	2 LA but not a list	21%	2 LA but not a list	17%	
	3 LA exchange	16%	3 LA exchange	14%	
Median distance moved	2-5 miles		2-5 miles		
Households Without Dependent Children	23		49		72
Row %	32.2%		67.8%		100.0%
Column %	28.8%		21.3%		23.1%
Mean age of HoH	43.4		49.7		
Main reasons for move	1 larger/better house	27%	1 family reasons	25%	
	2 smaller/cheaper house	26%	2 better area	20%	
% intending to buy	31%		9%		
How started renting?	1 waiting/transfer list	64%	1 waiting/transfer list	60%	
	2 LA but not a list	21%	2 LA but not a list	17%	
	3 LA exchange	16%	3 LA exchange	14%	
Median distance moved	Under 1 mile		1-2 miles		
Couples with dependent children	34		36		70
Row %	48.7%		51.3%		100.0%
Column %	42.5%		15.6%		22.5%
Mean age of HoH	30.9		33.3		
Main reasons for move	1 larger/better house	41%	1 large/better house	48%	
	2 better area	29%	2 family reasons	19%	
% intending to buy	28%		17%		
How started renting?	1 waiting/transfer list	69%	1 waiting/transfer list	52%	
	2 LA exchange	31%	2 LA exchange	30%	
	3	-	3 LA but not a list	15%	
Median distance moved	2-5 miles	-	2-5 miles		
Lone parents with dependent children	6		69		75
Row %	8.6%		91.4%		100.0%
Column %	7.5%		30.0%		24.3%
Mean age of HoH	34.0		28.4		
Main reasons for move	1 larger/better house	73%	1 larger/better house	35%	
	2 divorce/separation	14%	2 family reasons	25%	
% intending to buy	None		11%		
How started renting	1 LA but not a list	54%	1 waiting/transfer list	48%	
	2 waiting/transfer list	31%	2 LA exchange	28%	
	3 LA exchange	15%	3 LA but not a list	21%	
Median distance moved	Under 1 Mile		2-5 miles		
Totals	80		230*		310*
Column %	100.0%		100.0%		100.0%
Row %	25.8%		74.2%		10.0%

* figures may not sum correctly due to weighting and rounding.

Some support for the idea that a proportion of moves within the social rented sector might be accounted for by the desire of households to gain access to better accommodation within the sector prior to purchasing it through the 'right to buy' scheme is provided here. Single person households who were economically active were almost six times more likely than were those who were economically inactive (23 per cent compared to 4 per cent) to say that they intended to purchase their present accommodation at some time in the future.

After single person households, lone parents with dependent children accounted for the next largest proportion of movers. Almost one-quarter of moves by continuing households within the sector were by households of this type. Only 8.6 per cent of lone parent households were headed by someone who was economically active - a figure broadly consistent with other studies of the employment patterns of lone parents on low incomes (Bradshaw *et al.*, 1996). Lone parents with dependent children who are economically inactive represent 91.4 per cent of all moving lone parent households and 30.0 per cent of all moving households with an economically inactive head. The mean age of heads of household in this cell is 28.4 years and is the lowest for all types of household. The two main reasons given for moving by households of this type are, first, more suitable accommodation (ranked first by 35 per cent of all such households) and, second, 'family reasons' (ranked first by 25 per cent of all such households).

Almost 11 per cent of households in this cell state that they intend to try and the purchase the property at some time in the future. The most common 'route' into the accommodation was via a waiting or transfer list (in 48 per cent of cases), the second was via an 'exchange' of some kind (28 per cent of all cases) and the third most common was direct access via a local authority without being on a waiting or transfer list. The median distance over which such moves took place was between 2 to 5 miles.

Households without dependent children and couples with dependent children both account for about 23 per cent of all moves each. Couples with dependent children, with heads of household who are economically active or not, are on average significantly younger than are heads of households without dependent children. Households with economically active heads are also significantly more likely to be intending to purchase their new accommodation, adding weight to the proposition that a proportion of moves, especially amongst younger economically active households, are at least partially motivated by a desire to enter owner occupation via the 'right to buy' route.

Summary

This Chapter has attempted to describe patterns of residential mobility within the social rented sector. It has done this in two ways.

First, it has examined the characteristics of households in the social rented sector as a whole in order to establish if any factors significantly increase the chances of a household being mobile within the sector. Using techniques of logistic regression it was concluded that households headed by (i) younger people and (ii) households headed by someone who was economically inactive but which included dependent children, were significantly more likely to be mobile within the sector than were other household types. There was also some more limited evidence that rates of mobility within the sector were slightly higher in the South West than in the rest of England.

Second, it has also described the characteristics of mobile households in absolute terms. Mobile households were classified into eight main types on the basis of the economic status of their head of household and the structure of the household. The largest group of movers were older economically inactive single person households. Although the odds of this group moving, as revealed by the logistic regression analysis, were lower than for some other household types they still formed the largest group of movers because of the disproportionate number of them in the social rented sector. The second largest group were economically inactive lone parents, and the third largest group were households with an economically inactive head with dependent children. Movers with an economically active head were more likely to be intending to purchase the property they had moved into. The reasons for moving and the 'routes' into the new accommodation varied between the different types of moving household but by the far the most common reason for moving was the need for more suitable accommodation. The great majority of all moves by all household types were 'local'.

Chapter Three
Patterns of residential mobility amongst continuing households between the owner occupied sector and the social rented sector

Introduction

This Chapter attempts to describe the pattern of residential mobility amongst continuing households between the owner occupied sector and the social rented sector in England. Data from the SEH 1993/4 suggests that some 44 thousand continuing households left owner occupation and entered the social rented sector and some 35 thousand continuing households left the social rented sector and entered owner occupation - a net inflow of some 9 thousand continuing households.

The Chapter begins by examining the characteristics of households within the social rented sector which predispose certain households to leave it and enter owner occupation. It then examines the characteristics of households who have left owner occupation and entered social housing[15].

Which continuing households left the social rented sector for owner occupation?

This section contrasts the characteristics of those continuing households who were residentially mobile out of social housing into owner occupation with the characteristics of households who remained in the social rented sector. Table 3.1 (overleaf) presents the major differences.

---

[15] The number of cases available for analysis in this Chapter is small and, consequently, some of the analysis is based upon rather crude categories.

The mean age of the heads of household entering owner occupation was significantly (p<0.001) lower than the mean age of those remaining in the social rented sector. The mean age of those moving was just 36 years old whilst the mean age of those remaining was some 18 years greater than this. Those who were mobile were thus significantly younger than those remaining. Mobile households were also significantly more likely to be made up of married or cohabiting couples (p<0.001) and significantly more likely to contain two or more economically active adults (p<0.001). Over three-quarters of mobile households were based around couples compared to less than 40 per cent of households remaining in the social rented sector. A full two-thirds of mobile households contained two or more economically active adults compared to just 10 per cent of households who

Table 3.1
**The major differences in the socio-demographic characteristics of households
who had been residentially mobile into owner occupation from the social rented
sector compared to those who had remained in the social rented sector**

Socio-demographic characteristics	Households moving from the social rented sector into owner occupation N=35	Households remaining in the social rented sector N=4,439
Mean age of head of household	36 years***	54 years
Mean annual gross income of head of household and partner from all sources	£23,000***	£7,300
% of heads of household who were female	11.2%***	44.5%
% of households made up of married or cohabiting couples	76.0%***	38.0%
% of heads of household unemployed, retired or unable to work	10.4%***	72.4%
% of households containing at least two economically active adults	66.0%***	10.0%
% of households with a member who has previously been an owner occupier at some time in the past	17.2%	9.3%
% heads of household who are classified as minority ethnic group	9.1%	6.9%
% of heads of household in non-manual social class	35.8%	25.5%

Note: *** Differences significant at p < 0.001.

remained in the social rented sector. These significant differences in household structure and patterns of economic activity translate into significant differences in mean household incomes.[16] Whilst the mean gross annual income of the head of household and, if applicable, their partner, for households who were mobile, was almost £23,000 pounds, that for households who remained in the social rented sector was, at just under £7,300, less than one-third of this. Households who were mobile were significantly less likely to be headed by a female than were those who remained in the social rented sector (p<0.001) and they were also significantly much less likely to be headed by someone who was economically inactive.

Other differences were also apparent but not to such an extent to make them statistically significant. Mobile households were more likely to have heads from a non-manual social class background and were also more likely to have at least one household member who had, at some time in the past, previously been an owner occupier. Mobile households were also slightly more likely to be headed by a member of a minority ethnic group than were households who remained in the social rented sector.

Heads of household were asked what their main reasons were for moving. The most popular response was that they 'wanted to buy' (29 per cent), closely followed by wanting to move to 'a better area' (27 per cent). In only 6 per cent of cases had the move into owner occupation been primarily motivated by work related factors.

The great majority of moves had been over a short distance. Just over 35 per cent of all moves had occurred over a distance of less than two miles, just over 62 per cent had occurred over a distance of less than five miles, and almost 88 per cent had occurred over a distance of less than 10 miles. Thus, although households had left the social rented sector in order to enter owner occupation the great majority had done so whilst remaining within the same locality.

The initial outcomes of the move into owner occupation appeared to have been generally positive. Of those who had been mobile into owner occupation, over 97 per cent reported that they were either 'fairly' or 'very' satisfied with their new homes. This proportion compares with a figure of 93 per cent for all other owner occupiers and a figure of 80.6 per cent of all those in the social rented sector. Those who had been mobile into owner

---

16

    The figures given here have not been 'equivalised' in order to take account of the differences in household structures already identified (see Hills [1995] for details). Nevertheless the differences are such that even after this has been done large and significant differences will remain.

occupation from the social rented sector reported the highest levels of satisfaction with their accommodation of any group in the SEH.

Of those who had been mobile into owner occupation from the social rented sector, just over 10 per cent reported that they were already in arrears with their mortgage or were having difficulties making payments. However, the comparable figure of all other owner occupiers with a mortgage was some 19.7 per cent in 1993/4 (Burrows, 1997b). Thus, relative to all other mortgagors those recently mobile into owner occupation from the social rented sector were about half as likely to be facing problems of mortgage indebtedness.

Using the logistic regression framework outlined in the Appendix an attempt was made to model the odds of households being mobile out of the social rented sector into owner occupation. A wide range of variables was examined including those shown in Table 3.1. As already discussed the small number of cases leads to only very crude multivariate analyses being possible. Nevertheless the final 'best fitting' model arrived at, as shown in Table 3.2, is robust and provides a clear indication of the major factors which increase the odds of a household leaving social housing.

What does the model mean? First, the model suggests that as the age of the head of household increases, the odds of leaving social housing decrease significantly. Second, and

Table 3.2
'Best fitting' logistic regression model of the odds of a continuing
household leaving social housing and entering owner occupation

Base odds	0.003
Age	
16-44	1.00
45-64	0.27**
65+	0.14*
Economic status of head of household	
Inactive	1.00
Active	7.60**
Interaction effect 1	
Not	1.00
Couple*economically active	4.27**
Interaction effect 2	
Not	1.00
Dependent children*economically active	0.38*

* sig at p<0.05 ** sig at p<0.01
R_L^2 = 19.0%; Model Chi-Square = 82.51 sig at p<0.0001

as expected, it suggests that households with an economically active head are significantly more likely to move than are households with an inactive head, even after the influence of the other factors in the model are controlled for. However, the nature of association between mobility and the economic activity of the head is significantly mediated by two other factors. First, households based upon couples with an economically active head are even more likely to be mobile whilst, second, households containing dependent children with an economically active head are significantly less likely to be mobile. The model as a whole is able to account for about 19 per cent of the variation in the odds of mobility which, for data of this sort, is high.

Another way of expressing what the results are showing is to construct a Table which shows how any particular combination of household attributes impact upon the odds of mobility from social housing into owner occupation (the same procedure can be applied to any of the logistic regression results reported here). The overall (base) odds of a household moving in this way was estimated by the model to be just 0.003 (see Table 3.2). Table 3.3 shows how the base odds are influenced by different combinations of household structure, economic activity and the presence or otherwise of dependent children in the household for households where the head is aged between 16 and 44.[17]

It is clear that couples without dependent children with an economically active head are the most likely to be mobile, followed by couples with an economically active head with dependent children. Households with an economically active head not based upon couples are less likely to be mobile; those containing dependent children especially so.

Table 3.3
Estimated factors by which odds of mobility into owner occupation
from social housing is increased by different combinations of
household attributes for households with a head aged 16-44

Economic status of head of household	Economically inactive head of household		Economically active head of household	
Household based upon a couple?	Not couple	Couple	Not couple	Couple
No dependent children in household	1.0	1.0	7.6	32.5
Dependent children in household	1.0	1.0	2.9	12.3

---

[17]

These factors are derived by multiplying the parameter estimates shown in Table 3.2 which combine to define any particular cell in the manner already detailed in Chapter 2.

However, all households with an economically active head, whatever their structure and whether they contain dependent children or not, are more likely to have been mobile than households with an inactive head of household.

Which continuing households left owner occupation for the social rented sector?

Continuing households who left owner occupation for the social rented sector fall into two broad categories. First, households who were previously outright owners of their properties without any outstanding mortgage. Second, households containing younger members who, because of various factors, have found owning occupation unsustainable and have either had their property repossessed or have otherwise left owner occupation. Of the 44 thousand households the SEH estimates left owner occupation for the social rented sector in 1993/4 just under 40 per cent fell into the first category and just over 60 per cent fell into the second. Table 3.4 shows some of the main characteristics of the two groups compared to all households who remained in owner occupation, whilst Table 3.5 (p.28) compares the different routes into social housing for the two groups and their current levels of satisfaction with it.

Table 3.4 shows that the mean ages of the heads of household of each group differs significantly (p<0.001). Whilst the mean age of those still in owner occupation is 51 years, for those who entered social renting from outright ownership the mean age is considerably greater at 63 years, whilst for those who were previously mortgagors it is considerably younger at 41 years. These significant differences in age are indicative of different sets of forces 'pushing' and 'pulling' owner occupiers into social housing.

Table 3.4
Some differences in the socio-demographic characteristics of households entering social housing from outright ownership and owner occupation with a mortgage compared to all continuing owner occupiers

Characteristics	Those who previously owned outright N = 17	Those who were previously mortgagors N=26	All other households continuing in owner occupation N=13,448
Mean age of head of household	63***	41***	51
Current employment status of head of household %			
Employed full time	14.6	39.6	60.1
Employed part time	4.7	9.9	4.8
Unemployed	9.6	17.0	3.8
Retired	50.9	9.0	26.1
Unable to work	20.2	24.5	5.2
Household composition %			
Couple, with dependent children	9.4	25.0	24.0
Couple, without no dependent children	38.2	22.6	44.3
Lone parent	0.0	28.5	5.8
Complex adult household	0.0	0.0	2.9
Single male	15.6	7.9	9.7
Single female	36.8	16.0	13.4
Social class of head of household %			
I Professional	0.0	0.0	9.8
II Intermediate	41.4	19.6	33.4
IIIN Skilled non manual	21.9	28.8	14.3
IIIM Skilled manual	23.0	3.8	28.8
IV Semi skilled manual	13.7	3.4	10.8
V Unskilled manual	0.0	10.1	3.0
Mean annual gross income of head of household and partner from all sources	£6,935***	£11,375***	£18,960

*** Differences with all owner occupiers significant at p < 0.001.

Table 3.5
Routes into social housing from outright ownership and owner occupation with a mortgage and levels of satisfaction with current accommodation in the social rented sector

Characteristics	Those who previously owned outright N = 17	Those who were previously mortgagors N=26
How gained access to social housing?		
Via LA waiting list	61.0	27.4
Via LA not waiting list	26.6	25.2
Accepted as homeless	6.2	47.4
Some other way	6.2	0.0
Current status of previous owner occupied accommodation?		
Sold it	46.2	21.6
On market, trying to sell	26.1	7.3
Still owns, not on market	21.0	0.0
Previous partner still lives in it	0.0	8.7
Repossessed	0.0	62.4
Other eg demolished	6.7	0.0
Main reason for moving into social housing?		
Better area	0.0	4.3
Nearer job	0.0	3.7
Larger/better house	6.3	0.0
Smaller/cheaper house	11.9	3.4
Mortgage arrears	0.0	48.0
Divorce/separation	20.4	19.1
Family reasons	42.3	14.3
Personal reasons	0.0	3.6
Other	19.0	3.7
Proportion 'slightly' or 'very' dissatisfied with new social rented accommodation	20.9	31.2

One possible interpretation of the data is that older previously outright owners have made a 'strategic choice' to enter 'more suitable' social housing whilst the younger households have been 'forced' into social housing due to changed circumstances. Certainly, of the first group a high proportion (61 per cent) had gained access via local authority waiting lists after first selling (or attempting to sell) their previous homes (some 72 per cent). The majority of these movers, some 71 per cent, were either retired or otherwise economically inactive. Over a third (almost 37 per cent) were single females and over 38 per cent were couples with no dependent children. The most significant main reason given for entering social housing by this group was 'family reasons'. Almost 12 per cent of moves were due to wanting a smaller or a cheaper house. However, over 20 per cent of moves were due to divorce or separation. Given their socio-demographic characteristics it is possible that a large proportion of this group of movers were entering some form of 'sheltered' housing in the social rented sector.[18]

However, this 'strategic' interpretation might paint a rather rosier picture than the reality of the situation (McCafferty, 1994). An alternative interpretation of the data might be that such households are 'forced' into social renting because of the high costs of 'suitable' accommodation in the owner occupied sector. Some older people find owner occupation unsustainable and move to release equity and to have lower running costs. However, the options available tend to be very limited and some get offered social housing when that is not what they necessarily want (Oldman, 1991). Certainly, as Table 3.4 shows, the mean incomes of households in this group are low; lower even than the mean incomes of all households in social housing (see Table 3.1). It could be then that it is issues of affordability and the changing nature of their housing needs which have underpinned the bulk of this form of residential mobility. Older low income outright owners living in increasingly unsuitable homes might find that accommodation in the social rented sector is the only 'option' open to them.

There is possibly less ambiguity about interpretations of the motivations for residential mobility amongst the second group. As Table 3.4 shows, the majority of such households, over 51 per cent, are couples with children, or lone parents, and over 41 per cent of heads of household are either unemployed or otherwise economically inactive. As Table 3.5 shows almost one half of these households gained access to social housing by being accepted as homeless by their local authority. Over 60 per cent had lost their previous home due to repossession and almost 38 per cent had sold it. Almost one-half cited mortgage indebtedness as their main reason for moving into social housing.[19] The mean income of such households is significantly less than for owner occupiers as a whole but, as Table 3.1 shows, significantly greater than the mean income of all households in social housing.

The social class distribution of the head of household for both groups entering social housing from owner occupation differed markedly compared to the distribution of owner occupiers as a whole. As Table 3.4 shows, those from professional (social class I) backgrounds were absent in both groups. Amongst previously outright owners, those from

---

[18]   A clearer examination of this is possible using 1994/95 SEH data.

[19]   For a fuller analysis of this group see Ford (1997).

social classes II, IIIN and IV were over-represented and those from social classes IIIM and V were under-represented. Amongst those who were previously mortgagors, those from social classes IIIN, IIIM and V were over-represented and those from social classes II and IV under-represented.

The outcomes of such moves into social housing do not appear to be very satisfactory for either ex-outright owners or ex-mortgagors. Amongst all owner occupiers just 4.6 per cent of households reported that they were either 'slightly' or 'very' dissatisfied with their accommodation. However, as Table 3.5 shows, levels of dissatisfaction with accommodation amongst both groups of ex-owner occupiers was significantly greater than this. Almost 21 per cent of previously outright owners and over 31 of ex-mortgagors expressed dissatisfaction with their new accommodation in the social rented sector. Both of these figures also exceed levels of dissatisfaction in the social rented sector as a whole.

Finally, a logistic regression analysis was also carried out on the data but with so few cases only the crudest form of multivariate model was decipherable. The 'best fitting' model, shown in Table 3.6, suggests that the best predictors of a household leaving owner occupation for social housing are if the head of household is economically inactive and if the head of household is a lone parent.

Table 3.6
'Best fitting' logistic regression model predicting
if a household in owner occupation enters social housing

Base odds	0.002
Economic status of head of household	
Employed	1.00
Unemployed/unable to work	5.93***
Retired	1.82
Lone parent interaction	
Not	1.00
Single person household* dependent children	4.62***

*** sig at $p<0.01$
$R_L^2 = 6.0\%$; Model Chi-Square = 36.278 sig at $p<0.001$

Summary

This Chapter has shown a clear pattern of both continuing residualisation and social exclusion through an analysis of residential mobility between owner occupation and social housing. Essentially households with one or more of their members economically active have a markedly increased propensity to leave social housing and enter owner occupation.

Whilst households leaving owning occupation and entering social housing more often than not do so because they have found owner occupation unsustainable. Although the 'rate of exchange' of households between the two sectors is relatively small the 'direction' of change at the margins of the two tenures is clear enough.

Chapter Four
Patterns of residential mobility amongst continuing households between the private rented sector and the social rented sector

Introduction

This Chapter briefly describes the pattern of residential mobility amongst continuing households between the private rented sector (PRS) and the social rented sector in England. Data from the SEH 1993/4 suggest that some 67 thousand continuing households left the PRS and entered the social rented sector and some 31 thousand continuing households left the social rented sector and entered the private rented sector - a net inflow of some 36 thousand continuing households. The Chapter first examines the characteristics of the households who left the PRS and entered social housing and then the characteristics of those households who left social housing in order to enter the PRS.

Which continuing households from the private rented sector entered social housing?

This section examines the characteristics of continuing households who were residentially mobile between the PRS and social housing in 1993/4. Logistic regression models were fitted to the data in order to ascertain which variables best predicted that a household in the PRS would enter the social rented sector. The impact of a wide range of variables was examined and the final 'best fitting' model is shown in Table 4.1 (overleaf).

The results from this modelling exercise throw up few surprises. The odds of gaining access to social housing from the PRS are significantly increased if the head of household is economically inactive, if the household contains dependent children and if the head of household is from a manual social class background. Essentially then it is the most disadvantaged households who have dependent children who are the most likely to gain entry to social housing from the PRS.

Table 4.1
'Best fitting' logistic regression model for the
prediction of continuing household mobility from the PRS into social housing

Base Odds	0.01***
Economic status of head of household	
Active	1.00
Inactive	2.00*
Dependent children in household?	
No	1.00
Yes	2.34**
Social class of head of household	
Non manual social class	1.00
Manual social class	2.09*

* sig at p<0.05 ** sig at p<0.01
R_L^2 = 4.2%; Model Chi-Square = 19.581 sig at p<0.001

However, as we have discussed in previous Chapters, this form of analysis only tells us the odds of different household types being mobile. It does not detail the characteristics of mobile households in absolute terms. Given the relatively small number of cases available here, all we can do is to provide some simple descriptive statistics on some selected characteristics of mobile households. This is shown in Table 4.2 (opposite).

The Table shows that couples with no dependent children and single females form the two largest groups mobile into social housing from the PRS. However, and as already indicated in the modelling exercise, it is households with dependent children who are proportionately the most likely to follow this trajectory (lone parents especially so). This distinction between absolute proportions and relative odds of different households moving is a crucial one and is well illustrated by this example. The Table also shows that households headed by someone from a minority ethnic group background form almost 15 per cent of such household moves - although this variable 'drops out' of our 'best fitting' model when the other variables in the model are controlled for. In absolute terms it is households with a head who is employed full-time and households with a head who is unemployed which form the two largest group of movers (both at 27.9 per cent of all moving households). However, it is those who are headed by someone who is either unemployed or unable to work who are the more likely to have been residentially mobile. Finally, it is households with heads from skilled manual backgrounds who form the largest proportion of mobile households (43.1 per cent). In this instance it is also this household type which is most likely to have been mobile.

Table 4.2
Some selected characteristics of households who were
mobile from the PRS into the social rented sector

Variable	Mobile into Social housing % N=67	Stayed in the PRS % N=1927
Household structure		
Couple, no dependent children	25.4	24.6
Couple, with dependent children	19.4	13.4
Lone Parents with dependent children	13.4	5.5
Large adult household	3.0	13.6
Single male	17.9	22.8
Single female	20.9	20.1
Ethnic status of head of household		
White British	85.1	92.1
Minority ethnic	14.9	7.9
Economic status of head of household		
Employed full time	27.9	49.0
Employed part time	2.9	4.8
Unemployed	27.9	13.8
Retired	17.6	18.8
Unable to work	23.5	13.6
Social class of head of household		
I Professional	2.0	6.4
I Intermediate	13.7	28.4
IIIN Skilled non manual	13.7	15.6
IIIM Skilled manual	43.1	24.5
IV Semi skilled manual	17.6	18.2
V Unskilled manual	9.8	6.9

Table 4.3 (overleaf) shows data on the mechanisms by which continuing households from the PRS gained access to social housing, their main reasons for moving and the distance they moved. The majority gained access via a local authority waiting list (64.6 per cent), another 17.7 per cent via a local authority but not a through a list and just over 13 per cent gained access by being accepted as homeless by a local authority. Almost one-third of movers moved less than 2 miles, just over one-third moved between 2 but less than 5 miles and just under one-third moved five miles or more. The main reasons given for moving were: first, in order to gain more suitable accommodation (almost one-third of all movers); second, for 'family reasons'; third, because of the fact that their PRS accommodation was no longer available.

Table 4.3
Mechanisms of access to the social rented sector by continuing households
from the PRS; distances moved; and reasons for moving

Variable	% N=67
How did household gain entry to social housing?	
LA, waiting list	64.6
LA, not via list	17.7
Accepted as homeless	13.1
Other mechanism	4.6
Distance moved	
Under 1 mile	11.9
1 to less than 2 miles	20.9
2 to less than 5 miles	34.7
5 miles or more	32.5
Main reasons for moving	
More suitable accommodation	32.3
Family reasons	16.9
PRS accommodation no longer available	16.8
Personal reasons	8.7
Rent arrears	5.9
Other reasons	19.4

The levels of satisfaction with accommodation expressed by those households mobile into social housing from the PRS were not significantly different from those expressed by all households in the PRS. Of those households mobile into social housing 13.4 per cent said they were 'slightly' or 'very' dissatisfied with their new accommodation. This figure compared with 16.3 per cent of households expressing dissatisfaction in the PRS.

Some 16 per cent of households who moved into social housing from the PRS stated that they intended to try and purchase their new accommodation at some time in the future. However, almost 60 per cent of households mobile into social housing from the PRS stated that they intended to move out of the accommodation when they could.

Which continuing households from social housing entered the private rented sector?

The SEH contains only a very small number of households who were mobile into the PRS from the social rented sector making any general inferences difficult. Logistic regression analysis compared the characteristics of these movers with the characteristics of residents in social housing as a whole. The resulting 'best fitting' model is shown in Table 4.4.

Table 4.4
'Best fitting' logistic regression model predicting the odds of continuing households moving from social housing into the private rented sector

Base odds	0.01***
Age	
16-29	1.00
30-44	1.12
55-64	0.04**
65+	0.04***
Region	
Not East Anglia	1.00
East Anglia	7.50***
Single person household	
Not	1.00
Single person household	2.87**

** sig at $p<0.01$ *** sig at $p<0.001$
$R_L^2 = 14.9\%$; Model Chi-Square = 55.211 sig at $p<0.001$

This analysis suggests that the odds of moving out of social housing into the PRS decreases significantly with age. Single person households are the most likely to make such a move and the odds are also significantly increased for households living in East Anglia compared to the rest of the country.[20]

The three main reasons given for moving were (i) in order to gain more suitable accommodation (27.9 per cent) followed by (ii) 'family reasons' (27.0 per cent) and (iii) divorce or separation (14.4 per cent). Over 21 per cent of households expressed some dissatisfaction with their new accommodation - a proportion higher than that for both the PRS as a whole and the social rented sector as a whole.

---

[20]

The data do not allow us to say very much about this finding. However, as a working hypothesis it may be the case that given the rural character of this region such moves from social housing to the PRS may be related to the gaining of accommodation tied to agricultural employment (Bevan and Sanderling, 1996).

Summary

This Chapter has examined patterns of residential mobility by continuing households between the social rented sector and the PRS. The small number of cases available for analysis means that the results should be treated as suggestive rather than definitive. The analysis suggests that those households most likely to enter social housing from the PRS are more likely to be headed by someone who is economically inactive, more likely to contain a dependent child and more likely to come from a manual social class background. Households leaving social renting for the PRS are more likely than all households in social housing to be single person households and to be young. There is also some very limited evidence which suggests that such mobility may be more likely in rural than in urban areas.

Chapter Five
Residential mobility into social housing by new households

Introduction

Throughout this report a distinction has been made between the mobility of *continuing households* and that of *new households*. Chapters 2, 3 and 4 have dealt with patterns of residential mobility amongst continuing households. This Chapter examines the movements of new households in relation to social housing.

The 1993/4 SEH estimates that there were some 555 thousand new households formed in England who were residentially mobile. This total constituted about 26 per cent of all household moves. Of these moves by new households some 131 thousand (23.6 per cent) were into social housing, 206 thousand (37.1 per cent) were into owner occupation and 218 thousand (39.3 per cent) were into the private rented sector. This Chapter sets out to examine what factors, if any, differentiated the new households who entered social housing from those who entered owner occupation or the private rented sector. It then describes some of the main characteristics of new households entering social housing and contrasts these with the characteristics of households already living in the social rented sector.

In what ways do new households entering social housing differ from new households entering the other main tenures?

In order to answer this question the logistic regression framework utilised throughout this report was applied to the 1993/4 SEH data in order to model the odds of a new household entering social housing rather than owner occupation or the private rented sector.[21] To put

---

[21] Although not detailed here it is possible to contrast those entering social housing with those entering the two other main tenures separately by extending the logistic regression framework so that it can deal with three rather than two category dependent variables (Menard, 1995).

the analytic problem another way, we are asking what characteristics of newly formed households would best predict that they enter social housing rather than the other main tenures?

In order to investigate this question the relationship between the odds of new households entering social housing and a range of other variables was examined. All of the variables which displayed some form of significant bivariate association are shown in Table 5.1 (opposite). Also shown is the multivariate logistic regression model which 'best fitted' the data. We shall discuss the impact of each variable in turn and then offer an interpretation of the meaning of the 'best fitting' model.

The age of the head of a new household and the odds of entering social housing is broadly 'U' shaped. The chances are highest for both younger and older heads. Compared to those aged between 16 and 29 the only category where the odds are significantly increased is that of heads aged 65 and over. Further, this relationship holds in the 'best fitting' model even after the impact of age has been controlled for on the other variables in the model: the economic status of the head of household; household structure; region; and the social class of the head of the household. However, because the great majority of new households are young, in absolute terms the great majority of new households entering social housing are young.

The current economic status of the head of household has a marked impact on the odds of entering social housing. Compared to those who are employed full-time, the odds of entering social housing are significantly increased for all other categories of economic status, but especially for those who are currently economically inactive. The variable is the most important[22] to be included in the final 'best fitting' model. Those new households headed by someone who is currently unable to work or unemployed are the most likely to enter social housing even after controlling for age of the head of household; household structure; region; and social class of the head of household.

When examined on its own there appears to be an association between the ethnicity of the head of a new household and the odds of entering social housing. Specifically the data suggests that new households headed by someone who identifies themselves as 'West Indian' are over 3.5 times more likely to enter social housing than are new households headed by someone who identifies themselves as 'White British'. However, this association is not maintained when controlled for by the other variables considered here.

---

[22]

       The economic status of the head of household accounts for over half of the variation explained in the 'best fitting' model. Details of how to use logistic regression parameter estimates in order to estimate the relative impact of variables can be found in Menard (1995: 44-49).

Table 5.1
Logistic regression models of the odds of new households entering social housing

Variables	Bivariate	'Best fitting'
Base odds	Varies	0.03
Age of the head of household		
16-29	1.00	1.00
30-44	0.90	0.75
45-64	1.13	1.00
65+	3.23***	2.90*
Economic status of head of household		
Employed full time	1.00	1.00
Employed part time	3.22***	2.87***
Unemployed	6.48***	4.51***
Retired	6.80***	2.61*
Unable to work	7.76***	5.95***
Ethnicity of head of household		
White British	1.00	-
West Indian	3.58***	-
Indian	0.67	-
Pakistani/Bangladeshi	1.04	-
Other	1.26	-
Household structure		
Couple, no dependent children	1.00	1.00
Couple, with dependent children	1.98***	2.33***
Lone parents with dependent children	9.06***	3.60***
Large adult household	0.67	0.57
Single male	1.55**	1.07
Single female	2.59***	1.81**
Marital Status		
Married	1.00	-
Cohabiting	0.84	-
Single	1.09	-
Widowed	3.99***	-
Divorced or separated	2.65***	-
Region		
North	1.00	1.32
Yorkshire & Humberside	1.22	1.00
East Midlands	0.92	1.07
East Anglia	0.74	0.68
Greater London	0.84	1.03
Rest of South East	0.67***	0.66**
South West	0.71*	0.89
West Midlands	1.44*	2.01***
North West	1.37*	1.44**
Social class of head of household		
I Professional	1.00	1.00
II Intermediate	1.86	1.56
IIIN Skilled non manual	5.59***	2.58*
IIIM Skilled manual	8.95***	5.86***
IV Semi skilled manual	13.37***	6.06***
V Unskilled manual	22.65***	10.45***

* sig at $p<0.05$ ** sig at $p<0.01$ *** sig at $p<0.001$

For 'best fitting' model $R_L^2 = 25.6\%$; Model Chi-Square = 528.0 sig at $p<0.001$

This suggests that it is not ethnicity *per se* which increases the odds of entering social housing but the employment and household characteristics of West Indian headed households.

Differences in household structure have a significant impact on the odds of new households entering social housing. In particular, compared to couples with no dependent children (the new household type most likely to enter owner occupation), new households with dependent children (especially if they are lone parent households) are significantly more likely to enter social housing. The odds of single female households entering social housing is also significantly greater.

When considered on its own it appears as if the current marital status of the head of a new household influences the odds of the household entering social housing. In particular households headed by someone who is widowed, divorced or separated are significantly more likely to enter social housing than are new households headed by someone with a different marital status. However, when controlled for by the other variables the association does not hold. Thus, rather than marital status *per se* being the significant factor which increases the likelihood of a new household entering social housing, it is factors *associated* with becoming widowed, divorced or separated which are important. In particular the increased odds associated with ageing, economic status and, especially, household structure are likely to account for the reasons why marital status as a factor 'drops out' of the 'best fitting' model.

There is a clear regional impact upon the odds that a new household will enter social housing which is maintained even after controlling for: the age of the head of household; the economic status of the head of household; household structure; and the social class of the head of household. As elsewhere in this report this variable is treated in a slightly different way to the others in that, as explained in Chapter 2, contrasts are made in such a way that differences are calculated in relation to an 'overall' effect rather than in relation to some arbitrary reference group. The results suggest then that compared to England as a whole new households in the rest of the South East of England outside of Greater London (ROSE) are significantly less likely to enter social housing, whilst those in the North West and, especially, the West Midlands are significantly more likely to enter social housing. These results are broadly consistent with recent figures and maps published by Dorling (1995: 101-133) in his excellent *A New Social Atlas of Britain,* which attempt to examine patterns of housing demand and housing shortage in relation to social housing. These suggest that access to social housing for new households is likely to be most difficult in ROSE and least difficult in the urban areas of the North West and the West Midlands.

The association between the odds of entering social housing and the social class background of the heads of new households is highly significant. As might be expected the odds of entering social housing increase as one moves down the class structure. This relationship holds even after controlling for: age of head of household; economic status of head of household; household structure; and region. As would be expected, compared to new heads from a professional social class those heads from manual social class backgrounds are far more likely to enter social housing. The model estimates that new heads of households from skilled manual social class backgrounds are almost six times more likely, and those from unskilled manual class backgrounds over ten times more likely, than are those from professional class backgrounds to enter social housing.

Unlike some of the other models discussed in this report this one has a strong 'predictive' capacity. The main reason for this is that we are attempting to model a phenomenon which has a relatively good chance of occurring amongst new households. Of the 555 new households in the sample 131 entered social housing giving an odds of such an event occurring of 131/424, or 0.31. The 'best fitting' model is able to explain almost 26 per cent of the variation in the odds. And in almost 50 per cent of cases, knowledge of the age of head of household, the economic status of the head of household, the household structure, region and the social class of the head of household leads to a correct prediction that the household entered social housing.

The 'best fitting' model estimates that households with the combination of attributes which define the reference categories within the variables have an odds of entering social housing of 0.03. From the model it is possible to examine the predicted odds of a new household entering social housing with any combination of attributes which are in the model by multiplying this 0.03 figure by the correct factors. To take two extreme examples at opposite ends of the odds scale. First, the odds of a new household headed by someone aged 25, employed full-time, living in a household with a partner but no dependent children in the ROSE and coming from a professional social class background entering social housing are (0.03 x 1.00 x 1.00 x 1.00 x 0.66 x 1.00) 0.02[23]. Second, the odds of a new household headed by someone who is also 25 but unable to work due to the fact that they are living as a lone parent in the West Midlands, and have a semi-skilled manual class background, entering social housing are (0.03 x 1.00 x 5.95 x 3.60 x 2.01 x 6.06) 7.83.[24] The model thus estimates that the odds of the second household type entering social housing is almost 400 times greater than is the first.

---

[23]

        This is a probability of 0.2/(1+0.2) or 1.96%.

[24]

        This is a probability of 7.83/(1+7.83) or 88.67%.

This modelling exercise gives us a very clear indication of the relative chances households of different types have of entering social housing. The next section of the Chapter examines the characteristics of new households entering social housing and compares them with the characteristics of households already housed within the sector.

Do the characteristics of new households entering social housing significantly differ from the characteristics of households already housed in the sector?

In order to answer this question the characteristics of new households entering social housing are compared with the characteristics of households already in the sector. This is shown in Table 5.2. A number of quite stark differences between the two groups of households is apparent. Almost 72 per cent of new households are headed by someone aged between 16 and 29, compared to only 13.6 per cent of households in the sector as a whole. Whilst only 8.6 per cent of new households are headed by someone aged over 55, some 51.4 per cent of households in the sector as a whole are headed by someone in this age group.

In terms of household structure the figures show that lone parents are disproportionately over-represented amongst new households (forming 27.4 per cent of the total) whilst single females are disproportionately under-represented. As we shall see below however, these differences are largely explained by differences in the age profiles of the two groups of households.

There are some slight differences in the profile of the ethnicity of heads of household between the two groups. New households are less likely to be headed by someone who describes themselves as 'White British' than are households in the sector as a whole.

Heads of new households are also significantly more likely to be headed by someone who is unemployed or unable to work and significantly less likely to be headed by someone who is retired. Finally, there is little difference in the social class profile of the heads of new households, with only members of the armed forces being slightly over-represented amongst new households entering social housing compared to households already housed in the sector.

The moment that one controls for the huge age differences between the two groups of households most of the other differences disappear (logistic regression analysis not reported here). This is an important result analytically and from the point of view of policy. It suggests that rather than factors such as lone parenthood, economic inactivity and minority ethnic group membership *per se* being the characteristics which underpin the

Table 5.2
**Some selected characteristics of new households entering social housing
compared to households continuing to live in social housing**

Variable	New households entering social housing N=131 %	Households continuing in social housing N=4,308 %
Age		
16-29	71.9	13.6
45-54	15.6	22.9
45-54	3.9	12.2
55+	8.6	51.4
Household Structure		
Couple, no dependent children	17.5	23.5
Couple, with dependent children	18.0	15.1
Lone parents with dependent children	27.4	12.3
Large adult household	2.1	9.4
Single male	17.9	14.2
Single female	17.1	25.4
Ethnic status of head of household		
White British	86.3	93.3
West Indian	4.0	2.5
Indian	1.5	0.5
Pakistani/Bangladeshi	2.1	0.7
Other	6.0	2.9
Economic status of the head of household		
Employed full time	26.2	21.9
Employed part time	3.5	5.6
Unemployed	31.4	12.2
Retired	5.2	39.4
Unable to work	33.7	20.9
Social class of head of household		
I Professional	0.9	1.3
II Intermediate	10.7	10.4
IIIN Skilled non manual	14.6	13.4
IIIM Skilled manual	39.0	33.9
IV Semi skilled manual	20.0	25.9
V Unskilled manual	11.8	14.9
Armed forces	2.9	0.3

movement of new households into social housing, it is, in actuality, the fact that these characteristics are significantly over-represented amongst the young which is the real issue. It is young people who are disproportionately members of the new households entering social housing and they bring with them patterns of household formation, minority ethnic group membership and levels of economic inactivity which differentiate them from the older, more established, population within the social rented sector.

Summary

This Chapter examined the characteristics of new households who had recently moved into social housing. Compared to all new households, new households entering social housing were more likely to: be headed by someone who was aged either 16 to 29 or 65 or over; be headed by someone who is economically inactive; be headed by someone in a manual social class; contain dependent children; be located in the West Midlands or the North West. Compared to households already in the social rented sector, new households were significantly more likely to be headed by someone aged between 16 and 29 and, because of the characteristics of young adults, were more likely to be lone dependents, more likely to be unemployed and more likely to be a member of a minority ethnic group. The age profile of the heads of new households also meant that they were less likely to be retired.

Chapter Six
Some concluding remarks

At the beginning of this report it was argued that patterns of residential mobility were indicative of the direction of social change within both areas and tenures. If one 'reads' the patterns of mobility revealed in this report in this way the current 'direction' of change is strikingly clear.

The demographic profile of the population housed in the social rented sector has been fundamentally altered by the operation of Right to Buy. As is well established the 'exiting' into owner occupation via Right to Buy has primarily been made by middle-aged, usually married and economically active families. The middle of the age profile of the population in the social rented sector has been ripped out. As Figure 1.1 has shown, the age distribution of heads of household in the social rented sector is now bimodal with the larger of the two humps being centred around those in their mid 70s and the smaller of the two being centred around those in their mid 20s. As older tenants die they are generally being superseded by households with a much younger age profile. It is this feature of the population of the social rented sector which largely accounts for the observed increases in the rate of mobility within the sector.

Households within social housing with economically active heads, especially if they are households based around couples, are significantly more likely to leave the sector for owner occupation. However, due to the impact of the housing recession, in recent years increasing numbers of households have moved in the opposite direction as they have found owner occupation unsustainable. Households with heads who are unemployed or unable to work and lone parent households in particular have been forced out of owner occupation into the social rented sector. Very few people are currently leaving social housing for the PRS, but those who leave the PRS to enter social housing have very similar characteristics to new households entering social housing. They are disproportionately likely to be lone parents, economically inactive and from manual social class backgrounds. The new households entering social housing are significantly younger than existing tenants and are more likely to be economically excluded and to have dependent children.

Perhaps the most worrying feature of this ongoing process of social and spatial exclusion is the number of children that it involves. According to the SEH, although only 22.1 per cent of all households in the social rented sector are headed by someone who is in full-time employment (compared to 60.1 per cent of households in owner occupation and 49.0 per cent of households in the PRS) the social rented sector contains 26 per cent of all those aged under 16 years. The data presented in this report suggest that current patterns of residential mobility will lead to this proportion increasing.

The challenge to those working in the domain of housing policy is how best to respond to a complex set of demographic and socio-economic dynamics which have their roots in spheres well outside the locus of control of housing. It is clear that housing policy and innovative forms of housing management can only ever ameliorate but never solve the problem. The data reported in this report are the inexorable results of processes of economic restructuring and social polarisation which have come to predominate life in contemporary Britain over the past two decades. The most convincing account of the new 'human ecology' which has resulted has been provided by Mike Davis (1990; 1992; Burrows, 1997a). He presents a stark picture of the development of a new form of 'spatial partitioning' within which the socially excluded are also increasingly spatially excluded (see also Hoggett [1994]). Given what we already know about the spatial distribution of current social housing, (Dorling, 1995: 106-133), the analysis of residential mobility in relation to social housing is thus increasingly an analysis of a form of exclusion which is at one and the same time both social and spatial. As indicated in the introduction to this report, that data suggests that social housing is increasingly the destination for those sections of the population 'funnelled' towards it (Lee et al., 1995: 45) by the exclusionary pressures invoked by the (post-Fordist) restructuring of the economy and the welfare state over the last decade and a half (Burrows and Loader, 1994). Others still are funnelled past it on to the streets (Burrows et al., 1997).

References

Bevan, M. and Sanderling, L. (1996) *Private Renting in Rural Areas*, Centre for Housing Policy Research Report, University of York: Centre for Housing Policy.

Bines, W., Kemp, P., Pleace, N. and Radley, C. (1993) *Managing Social Housing*, London: HMSO.

Boyle, P. (1995) 'Public Housing as a Barrier to Long-Distance Migration', *International Journal of Population Geography*, Vol. 1, 147-164.

Bradshaw, J., Kennedy, S., Kilkey, M., Hutton, S., Corden, A., Eardley, T., Holmes, H. and Neale, J. (1996) *The Employment of Lone Parents: A Comparison of Policy in 20 Countries,* London: Family Policy Studies Centre.

Buck, N. (1994) 'Housing and Residential Mobility' in N. Buck *et al.* (eds) *Changing Households: the British Household Panel Survey 1990-92,* ESRC Research Centre on Micro-Social Change, University of Essex.

Buck, N. (1996) *Using Panel Surveys to Study Migration and Residential Mobility,* University of Essex: ESRC Research Centre on Micro-Social Change.

Burrows, R. (1997a) 'Virtual Culture, Urban Social Polarisation and Social Science Fiction' in B. Loader (ed) *The Governance of Cyberspace,* London: Routledge.

Burrows, R. (1997b) 'Mortgage Indebtedness in England: An "Epidemiology"', *Housing Studies*, 12, 4, Forthcoming.

Burrows, R. and Loader, B. (eds) (1994) *Towards a Post Fordist Welfare State?* London: Routledge.

Burrows, R., Pleace, N. and Quilgars, D. (eds) (1997) *Homelessness and Social Policy,* London: Routledge.

Butler, T. (1995) 'Gentrification and the Urban Middle Classes', in T.Butler and M.Savage (eds) *Social Change and the Middle Classes,* London: UCL Press.

Campbell, B. (1993) *Goliath: Britain's Dangerous Places,* London: Methuen.

Carlen, P. (1996) *Jigsaw: A Political Criminology of Youth Homelessness,* Buckingham: Open University Press.

Champion, T. and Fielding, T. (eds) (1992) *Migration Processes and Patterns: Volume 1 Research Progress and Prospects,* London: Belhaven.

Davis, M. (1990) *City of Quartz,* London: Verso.

Davis, M. (1992) *Beyond Blade Runner: Urban Control, the Ecology of Fear,* Westfield, NJ: Open Magazine Pamphlets.

Department of the Environment (1993) *Housing in England: Housing Trailers to the 1988 and 1991 Labour Force Surveys,* London: HMSO.

Dorling, D. (1995) *A New Social Atlas of Britain,* London: Wiley.

Durrant, C. and Taper, T. (1995) *An Evaluation of HOMES,* London: Department of Environment.

Featherstone, M. (1995) *Undoing Culture: Globalization, Postmodernism and Identity,* London: Sage.

Ford, J. (1997) 'Mortgage Arrears, Mortgage Possessions and Homelessness' in R.Burrows, N.Pleace and D.Quilgars (eds) *Homelessness and Social Policy,* London: Routledge.

Forrest, R. and Murie, A. (1983) 'Residualisation and Council Housing: Aspects of the Changing Social Relations of Tenure' *Journal of Social Policy,* 12, 4, 453-468.

Forrest, R. and Murie, A. (1990a) *Selling the Welfare State,* London: Routledge.

Forrest, R. and Murie, A. (1990b) *Residualisation and Council Housing: a Statistical Update,* Bristol: School of Advanced Urban Studies.

Forrest, R. and Murie, A. (1992) 'Housing as a Barrier to the Geographical Mobility of Labour' in T. Champion and T. Fielding (eds) (1992) *Migration Processes and Patterns: Volume 1 Research Progress and Prospects,* London: Belhaven.

Forrest, R. and Murie, A. (1994a) 'Residential Mobility, Housing Exclusion and Social Stratification in Britain: Some Research Evidence', Paper Presented to the International Sociological Association Conference, Bielefield.

Forrest, R. and Murie, A. (1994b) 'Home Ownership in Recession', *Housing Studies,* 9, 1, 55-74.

Forrest, R., Murie, A., Doogan, K. and Burton, P. (1991) *Labour Mobility and Housing Provision: A Review of the Literature,* University of Bristol: School of Advanced Urban Studies.

Gilbert, N. (1993) *Analyzing Tabular Data: Loglinear and Logistic Models for Social Researchers,* London: UCL Press.

Green, H. and Hansbro, J. (1995) *Housing in England 1993/4: A Report of the 1993/4 Survey of English Housing,* London: HMSO

Green, H., Thomas, M., Iles, N. and Down, D. (1996) *Housing in England 1994/5: A Report of the 1994/5 Survey of English Housing,* London: HMSO.

Hills, J. (1995) *Joseph Rowntree Foundation Inquiry into Income and Wealth* (Volume 2), York: Joseph Rowntree Foundation.

Hoggett, P. (1994) 'The Politics of the Modernisation of the UK Welfare State' in R. Burrows and B. Loader (eds) *Towards a Post-Fordist Welfare State?* London: Routledge.

Holmans, A. (1996) 'Leaving Home and Household Formation' in H. Green, M. Thomas, N. Iles and D. Down (1996) *Housing in England 1994/5: A Report of the 1994/5 Survey of English Housing,* London: HMSO.

Institute of Fiscal Studies (1996) *Living With the State* - Executive Summary, London: IFS.

Lash, S. and Urry, J. (1994) *Economies of Signs and Space,* London: Sage.

Lee, P., Murie, A., Marsh, A. and Riseborough, M. (1995) *The Price of Social Exclusion,* London: NFHA.

Maclennan, D. and Kay, H. (1994) *Moving on, Crossing Divides: A Report on Policies and Procedures for Tenants Transferring in Local Authorities and Housing Associations,* Deptartment of the Environment, London: HMSO.

McCafferty, P. (1994) *Living Independently: a Study of the Housing Needs of Elderly and Disabled People,* London: HMSO.

McGregor, A., Munro, M., Heafey, M. and Symon, P. (1992) *Moving Job, Moving House: The Impact of Housing on Long-Distance Labour Mobility,* University of Glasgow Centre for Housing Research Discussion paper No. 38.

Menard, S. (1995) *Applied Logistic Regression Analysis,* London: Sage.

Oldman, C. (1991) 'The Financial Effects of Moving in Old Age', *Housing Studies,* 6, 4, 251-262.

Page, D. (1993) *Building for Communities,* York: Joseph Rowntree Foundation.

Power, A. (1994) *Area Based Poverty, Social Problems and Resident Empowerment,* London School of Economics: STICERD Discussion Paper 107.

Power, A. and Tunstall, R. (1995) *Swimming Against the Tide: Polarisation or Progress on 20 Unpopular Council Estates, 1980-1995,* York: Joseph Rowntree Foundation.

Prescott-Clarke, P., Clemens, S. and Park, A. (1994) *Routes into Local Authority Housing: A Study of Local Authority Waiting Lists and New Tenancies,* Department of Environment, London: HMSO.

Prior, L. (1995) 'Chance and Modernity: Accidents as a Public Health Problem' in R. Bunton, S. Nettleton and R. Burrows (eds) *The Sociology of Health Promotion: Critical Analyses of Consumption, Lifestyle and Risk,* London: Routledge.

Room, G. (ed) (1995) *Beyond the Threshold: the Measurement and Analysis of Social Exclusion,* Bristol: Policy Press.

Speak, S., Cameron, T., Woods, R. and Gilroy, R. (1995) *Young Single Mothers: Barriers to Independent Living,* London: Family Policy Studies Centre.

Vincent, J., Deacon, A. and Walker, R. (1993) *Security, Variety and Glorious Uncertainty: the Experiences of ex-Alvaston Resettlement Residents,* Centre for Research in Social Policy, Loughborough: Loughborough University of Technology.

Watt, P. (1996) 'Social Stratification and Housing Mobility', *Sociology*, 30, 3, 533-550.

Wilcox, S. (1995) *Housing Finance Review 1995/6,* York: Joseph Rowntree Foundation.

Appendix
Using logistic regression to analyse the odds of residential mobility

It is highly unlikely that the 'risk' or 'chance' of being residentially mobile will be evenly distributed across all households. It is much more likely that the likelihood of moving house in any year will be associated with a complex range of factors. The aim of multivariate statistical analysis within this context is to begin to disentangle these factors and to estimate what relative importance should be attached to each. This can most usefully be done by using a technique known as logistic regression to model the odds of mobility (Menard, 1995).

Those familiar with the mathematics of horse racing will recognise the odds of an event to be simply another way of expressing a probability that it will occur. Consider the data in Table A.1 for example. It shows the relationship between the current economic status of all heads of continuing households (HoH) in the social rented sector and whether or not they were residentially mobile in the last year.

For all continuing households currently in the social rented sector some 7 per cent (310/4424) moved within the sector in the past year. However, as the Table shows, this proportion varied in relation to the current economic status of the head of the household. So, for example, of those continuing households with a retired head only 3.2 per cent (55/1697) of households moved, whilst 12.1 per cent (114/941) of continuing households with a head unable to work did so. As is familiar, these *proportions* are given by the ratio of the number of households in such a position divided by the total number of households. The *odds* of moving for different household types is simply another way of expressing these proportions. The odds is given by the ratio of the number of households *who have moved* divided by the number of households *who have not moved*. So, for example, the odds of all households moving is given by 310/4114, for those with retired heads it is given by 55/1642 and for those with heads unable to work it is given by 114/827.

More generally, the odds of an event is given by p/(1-p) where p is the probability of an event occurring (and therefore, it follows, the probability is given by o/(1+o) where o is the odds of an event occurring). As Prior (1995) has recently pointed out, in this highly individualistic age there is a widespread tendency to attach probabilities, odds, or other indicators of risk, to individuals or, in this case, individual households. It is as if each *individual or household* possesses some given predisposition towards various conditions: illness; accidents; or, in this case, residential mobility. This is, of course, a nonsense. Probabilities can only ever be understood in terms of *collective* social properties. It is important to bear this in mind. Although the language used may sometimes indicate otherwise, the odds associated with the characteristics of any given collective social group should not be imputed to any single individual or household.

Table A.1
Current economic status of continuing heads of household in the social rented sector by whether household has moved or not in the last year

Economic Status of HoH	Employed full time	Employed part time	Unem-ployed	Retired	Unable to work	Total
Non mover Col %	912 93.2%	231 94.2%	502 89.1%	1642 96.8%	827 87.9%	4114 93.0%
Mover Col %	66 6.8%	14 5.8%	61 10.9%	55 3.2%	114 12.1%	310 7.0%
Total	978 100%	246* 100%	563 100%	1697 100%	941 100%	4424 100%

*Numbers may not sum correctly due to weighting and rounding.

Bivariate logistic regression results provide little more than a shorthand way of examining associations within a simple crosstabulation. Each individual category of a variable is compared to a selected 'reference' category of the variable and a measure of the difference between the odds of moving and not moving is calculated between the two categories. To take the example of the data already discussed in Table A.1, when this is analysed using logistic regression the results shown in Table A.2 are produced.

Table A.2
Bivariate logistic regression model of the odds of continuing households moving within the social rented sector using current employment status of the head of household as a predictor

Variable	Estimated odds
Base odds	1.20
Current employment status of the HoH	
Employed full time	1.00
Employed part time	0.85
Unemployed	1.69***
Retired	0.46***
Unable to work	1.91***

** sig. at p<0.01) *** sig. at p<0.001
R_L^2 = 4.0%; Model Chi-Square = 90.106, sig at p<0.001

This model estimates the odds of moving for different categories of employment status. Each category is compared to an arbitrary 'reference category' - in this case heads of household who are employed full-time. Thus, each estimated odds shows how much more or less likely a particular employment category is to invoke a household move. So, for example, the model estimates that compared to households with a head who is employed full-time, households with a head who is unemployed are 1.69 times more likely to move; those with a head who is unable to work are 1.91 times more likely; and those with a head who is retired are over two times *less* likely to move[1] (all sig at p <0.001). Those households with heads employed part-time are estimated to be 0.85 times as likely (that is 1.17 times less likely) to move than are households with heads employed full-time. However, this estimate is not statistically significant and so there is not enough evidence to suggest that the odds differ from households with heads employed full-time.

The model chi-square figure shows that knowledge of the employment status of the head of a household in the social rented sector significantly (p<0.001) increases our ability to predict whether or not the household is likely to have been residentially mobile or not in the last year. The R_L^2 figure (sometimes known as a pseudo coefficient of determination for logistic regression) gives an estimate of how well the model is able to predict the odds that a household has been mobile in the last year. In this case the figure of 4 per cent means that knowledge of the employment status of a head of household accounts for about

---

[1] An estimated odds of less than 1.00 suggests that the chance of an event occurring is decreased. So the figure of 0.46 means that a move is less likely to occur. It follows then that the reciprocal of this figure (1/0.46 = 2.17) gives an indication of how many times less likely.

4 per cent of the variation of the odds of a household moving. A figure for R_L^2 of 100 per cent would mean that knowledge of one variable would allow for perfect prediction of the other whilst a figure for R_L^2 of 0.0 per cent would mean that knowledge of one variable would not help in predicting another at all.

Some caution should be exercised when interpreting these figures, and the ones which follow, in terms of *relative risk*. The odds ratio is similar, but not identical, to relative risk. Further, when the prevalence of an outcome is high, logistic regression models can provide inaccurate estimates. Given this it is perhaps better to interpret estimates for odds as if they were on an ordinal rather than a ratio scale. So, although we can be confident that a parameter estimate of 1.91 is greater than a parameter estimate of 0.46, we cannot be quite so confident that it is exactly 4.15 times as great (1.91/0.46).

The great advantage of logistic regression for our analysis here is that it allows us to explore if bivariate associations are spurious in a manner which is much less clumsy than that possible using complex crosstabluations. It also allows us to explore associations between variables at different levels of measurement such as the association between the odds of moving (a dichotomy) and age (an interval level variable). Although the appearance of an association between two variables may appear to be robust it can often be an artefact (or a byproduct) of other factors 'working through' the bivariate association. Indeed, this problem of spuriousness provides the very basis for the necessity of doing multivariate analysis in the first place.

To take a simple example, we might hypothesise that the age of a head of household and the odds of moving will be associated. Using logistic regression we can explore what the nature of this association is and what impact, if any, it has on the nature of the association with the employment status of the head of household. In essence, we are able to examine the influence of employment status on the odds of moving after controlling for the influence of age.[2] The results of this are shown in Table A.3.

These results suggest that after controlling for the age of the head of household (entered as a continuous variable) the nature of the association between the employment status of the head of household and the odds of residential mobility is fundamentally altered. The model estimates that as the age of a head of household increases, the odds of the household moving decreases, at an average rate of 0.05 per year of age (this is the meaning of the 0.95 figure). Thus, the older the head of household the less is the likelihood of the household moving. Once the influence of age has been removed from the impact of employment status a very different picture is revealed from that suggested

---

2

Which also means of course that we can examine the influence of age after controlling for the influence of employment status.

in the bivariate analysis summarised in Table 2.3. Compared to households headed by someone who is employed full-time the only categories which significantly differ are those for households headed by someone who is retired (estimated to be 2.42 times more likely to move) or unable to work (estimated to be 1.95 times more likely to move).

Table A.3
Logistic regression model of the odds of continuing households moving within the social rented sector using current employment status and age of the head of household as predictors

Variable	Estimated odds
Base odds	0.43
Current employment status of the HoH	
Employed full time	1.00
Employed part time	1.00
Unemployed	1.43
Retired	2.42**
Unable to work	1.95***
Age of head of household	0.95***

** sig. at $p<0.01$) *** sig. at $p<0.001$

$R_L^2 = 6.5\%$ Model Chi-Square = 145.756, sig at $p<0.0001$

One can continue adding variables in this way in order to examine the relative influences of combinations of different variables. Variables may be considered in terms of the influence they have operating on their own or in combination with other variables. The combined effect of variables is know as an 'interaction' effect. This refers to the notion that some social factors only have an influence when they occur in combination with another factor. In exploratory analyses of the sort which underpin the analysis here the general aim is to establish models which 'best fit' the data (to use the statistical terminology). That is to say the aim is to select the combination of variables (which on *a priori* grounds one might suspect are associated with housing mobility) which maximise the predictive[3] capabilities of the model whilst at the same time making theoretical sense. In this process variables themselves may also sometimes be collapsed in order to more fully draw out the main differences between categories. For example in Table 2.4 it is

---

[3]

The level of the predictive power of models in the social and policy sciences tends, in general, to be low. In most cases then we are less interested in how well we can predict phenomena than we are in trying to establish which factors significantly increase or decrease the odds of some event - in this case residential mobility - occurring. In much of the analysis which follows in this report the emphasis will be on discussion of individual parameter estimates within models rather than on the overall R_L^2.

clear that the five categories of employment status could be collapsed into two categories - for those who are economically *active* (employed full-time and part-time) and for those who are economically *inactive* (unemployed, retired or unable to work) - in order to draw out sharper distinctions. This whole process of refining models in order to maximise predictive capacity whilst at the same time attempting to simplify variables and maintain theoretical coherence is known in the literature as striving for the most 'parsimonious' model (Gilbert, 1993) - that is, constructing the simplest model which is also theoretically intelligible.

One final complication to note is that there are a number of ways in which comparisons can be made between the effects of each category in a variable. Here discussion of the results will usually be in relation to an indicated 'reference category' within each variable because this the simplest way of interpreting the influence of nominal level variables. Thus, all significant differences are differences in relation to a stated reference category or, to use the argot, 'paradigmatic' instance. An alternative way of expressing the results would be to examine the deviations of each odds ratio for each category of a variable in relation to the overall effect of the variable. This would have the advantage of providing us with a global test of heterogeneity between the odds ratios - that is, it implicitly asks can the hypothesis that they all came from a population of sub-groups with a common level of risk be rejected? However, the interpretation of such deviations in relation to some abstract overall 'variable effect' is more difficult to decipher than deviations calculated in relation to a more concrete 'paradigmatic' person and/or household. Consequently this procedure is only used when considering regional differences where such a conceptualisation of differences makes more intuitive sense than the alternative (i.e. does living in a particular region influence the odds compared to England as a whole?).